BEING AND SOMETHINGNESS

RED EGG

BY
JEAN BONNIN

Also by Jean Bonnin

Novels:

A Certain Experience of the Impossible (2009)

Lines Within The Circle (2012)

The Cubist's House (2016)

Poetry, Essays and Articles:

Un-usual Muse-uals (2012)

Translations:

Sens Magique – by Malcolm de Chazal (2016)

Jean Bonnin

Jean Bonnin was born in Lavaur, in the Tarn in France,
in the year of the deep snows; he was brought up mainly
in Wales and England. He took his first degree in
government and politics at Birmingham, and his second
in political philosophy at Hull; his doctoral research was
on the theories of despotism. After university he lived and
worked in France, Portugal, Ireland, and the former
East Germany. On deciding to leave the underground and
avant-garde music scenes of Berlin and northern France behind
him – but not to abandon his music-making altogether –
he returned to Wales to concentrate on his writing
and his artwork. And Wales is where he now lives in
his empty house save for his lobster unicycle
and the Malcolm de Chazal painting
above his fireplace.

Being and Somethingness

An Original Publication of Black Egg Publishing

An imprint of Red Egg International

First published in the UK by Red Egg Publishing

in 2015

www.redeggpublishing.com

RED **EGG**

Copyright © Jean Bonnin 2015

Jean Bonnin has asserted his moral right to be identified as the author of this book

Cover design: Red Egg Publishing

British Library Cataloguing-in-Publication Data

A catalogue record for this book is available upon

request from the British Library

ISBN: 978-0-9571258-3-4

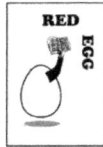

BEING AND
SOMETHINGNESS

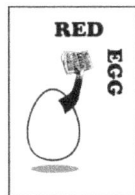

RED EGG

BY
JEAN BONNIN

INTRODUCTION

The idea for this book, and its subsequent creation, came from five coinciding, yet distinct, elements:

Firstly, *la théorie de l'obscurité* was obliquely employed to ascertain whether or not this was indeed a worthy project – worthy of both its name and its intentions. *La théorie de l'obscurité* states that the existence of a creative piece of work must be completely forgotten (and subsequently recalled or stumbled upon) before it can be deemed to have any artistic significance whatsoever. And this was the case with *Being and Somethingness*; being, as it was, (intentionally) discarded seventeen years ago, proverbially wrapped up and disguised as something completely different – (See end section, *Non-Scientific*, for further more accurate details).

Secondly, was my application of the 'stick together' technique of writing, necessarily combined with a certain degree of aleatoricism. Most of the results that arose from the employment of these techniques, however, were necessarily and even obligatorily set aside (more specifically, they were swathed in waterproof material, attached to a heavy rock and dropped into the well at the bottom of my field. And will only be retrieved after *la théorie de l'obscurité* has once again truly fulfilled its function and I have utterly forgotten about the document's existence also [or equally it could be there forever]).

If, however, in several years' time while taking in the crisp autumn air I stroll past my deep deep well and happen to recall the document at the foot of my borehole then these dalliances could quite possibly end up being published in the sequel to this volume. Nonetheless, these techniques did influence, no matter how marginally, this book.

Thirdly, *Being and Somethingness* to some degree emerges out of a belief that everything is interconnected. Sound and vision, movement and laughter, colour, plants and animals are all distinct and separate only because that is how man in more recent times has decided to classify his world. But is this truly the case or only one manner of interpretation in an otherwise much more homogenous atomistic universe?

Fourthly, a sideways smirk, grimace and consequent nod of acknowledgement must go to both Jean-Paul Sartre, for obvious reasons, as well as to the Welsh surrealist movement.

Fifthly, and finally, an influence upon this work has also been my initial discovery and subsequent long association, appreciation and comprehension of the works and world of the artist and writer Malcolm de Chazal… However, that said, I would not wish there to be any misinterpretation: the writing to be found here should not be seen as having any direct correlation with the superb and alchemical works of Monsieur de Chazal himself. These are my own short poems, aphorisms, perspectives, what you will, which I present to the reader as a completely original piece of work.

Here then is:

BEING AND SOMETHINGNESS.

BEING AND SOMETHINGNESS

BY

JEAN BONNIN

1.

The golden rain
Balances
On the autumn leaf
And awaits
The fall of winter.

2.

The holes in the sky
Are shaped like stars.
Pinpricked light
From the galaxies
Beyond.

3.

Inside the mirror
Out of sight
Happy people
Are dancing.

4.

Clocks have
Nothing
To do
With time.

5.

The lake
Swallows the moon
And spits out stars.

6.

Clockwise and
Anti-clockwise
Hold a secret
Rendezvous
At six o'clock.

7.

The giant eyeball
In the cage
Sees everything
And says nothing.

8.

Spoons
Are hollows
For gathering
Liquid thoughts.

9.

Good love
From a bad woman
Is better than
Bad love
From a good woman.

10.

When blue
And red
Shake hands
Purple
Takes a bow.

11.

Wind is the messenger
Of the skies.

12.

Preoccupations
Ring the bell
In the hotel lobby
Of the mind.

13.

Infinity
Is endless.
But reversed
You arrive
At zero.

14.

The walls have ears
The windows have eyes
And the door a mouth.

15.

When red
Was red with anger
It set alight.

16.

Sailors
Swill their rum
In the early
Morning sun.

17.

The waterfall
Sings
To the tune
Of gravity's
Light.

18.

The tired yawn
Drinks coffee.

19.

Red danced
With white
And turned
Pink.

20.

The alter ego
Of alter ego
Is man.

21.

The dark side
Of the earth
Sleeps
Till sunrise.

22.

Sometimes I feel my doppelgänger
In a parallel universe
Is thinking of me.

23.

Only madmen
Sing in vacuums.

24.

The Antipodes
Is where all
The spare sky
Is stored.

24.

When purple
Turned purple
With rage
Blue calmed it down.

25.

When green
Was green
With envy
It exploded.

26.

Daylight tucks
Night into
Bed.

27.

The circle
Bounces
Around
The Cubist
With glee.

28.

Footsteps
Reveal
Direction
But not
Intention.

29.

Time machines
Are possible
In the future
And in the past
But not right
Now.

30.

The world
In winter
Disappears.
It is only
Its memory
On our eyes
That make it
Appear as if
It's still there.

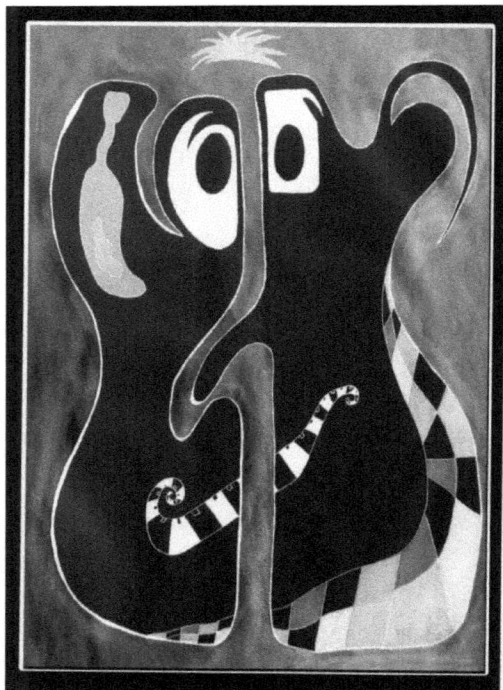

31.

The world
Is
Upside down
And
We are
On our
Heads.

32.

If the fullness
Of emptiness
Is emptied out
You have
Space.

33.

The tail
Is chasing
The barking
Dog in circles.

34.

The mouth
Of the volcano
Kisses the sky.

35.

Always be precise
About your inexactitudes.

36.

If it's your tongue
On the tip
Of your tongue
Do you become
Forgetful?

37.

In the hotel
Infinity
A room
Can always
Be made
Available.

38.

Reflections make us
Look at the world backwards
But glimpse the world sideways.

39.

Mountains
Pierce the sky
So that
On the other side
They are valleys.

40.

Only fortune
Can save us
From misfortune
Only adventure
Can save us
From misadventure
Only our self
Can save us from
Ourselves.

41.

Matter
Becomes
Doesn't matter
Becomes
Anti-matter.

42.

The doors
To heaven and hell
Are closed
With padlocks.
The keys
Are somewhere
On earth.

43.

The chicken
Said to
The egg:
"You used
To be
Square."

44.

The path
To infinity
Looks
Laughs
And knows
We should
Take
A different
Route.

45.

To go
Beyond
Dada
Is to
Time-travel.

46.

A round table
Pushed up
Into
The corner
Of a room
Is like
Man
In the
Universe.

47.

If the sky
Were green
And the grass
Blue
What difference
Would
That make?

48.

In the future
Everyone
Will be
Anonymous
For fifteen
Minutes.

49.

Tongue-in-cheek
Is a joke
Told sideways.

50.

A stitch
In time
Is sewn
Into
The fabric
Of space.

51.

Paper tigers live
In cardboard jungles.

52.

Some people
Communicate
Nothing
About
Everything.

53.

Thoughts are
The inaccurate
Melding
Of space-time
With the mind.

54.

To remain still
On a spinning
Ball
You have
To
Move
Very quickly.

55.

Love lost
Is love
Gained
To the power
Of minus
Two.

56.

The universe
Is infinite
As is
Man's desire
To disprove
This fact.

57.

Surrealism
Is the gateway
To the
Metaphysical.

58.

The cubist's
House
Has secret
Corners.

59.

The bicycle
Is static.
The road
Is being
Pulled along
By an
Invisible
Hand.

60.

A dagger
Held to the
Heart
Reveals
More truth
Than the offering
Of a thousand
Red
Roses.

61.

The door
Makes
A knocking
Sound
So as not
To be
Ignored.

62.

The clouds
Today
Are Puffs
From
A giant
Pipe.

63.

If a
Joke
Is told
In a
Forest
And nobody
Laughs
Is it really
A joke?

64.

Mirrors
Placed opposite
Each other
Quietly
Reflect
Upon the
Nature
Of infinity.

65.

At night
The speed of
Light sleeps
With
One eye
Open.

66.

If birds flew
Upside-down
The universe
Would be
At their feet.

67.

Each time
She cut me
With her words
I retaliated
By saying nothing.

68.

The pencil
Is mightier
Than the bomb.

69.

Love in colder
Climates
Is a necessity.

70.

Prawns
Are pink
Because
Of something
They said.

71.

Since
There is
No question
The telephone
Remains
Unanswered.

72.

The dotted
Line
Is the artist's
Morse code.

73.

Walls are
Hopeless
Constructs
Of the
Fearful
Mind.

74.

Love
Lingered
Lost.

75.

The lost
Ball
Floats
Upon
The endless
Water.

76.

Envelopes
Only
Laugh
Once.

77.

On the
Last day
Everybody
Slept.

78.

He who
Laughs last
May be
Anticipating
Something.

79.

Starfish
Are
Extra-terrestrials
That have fallen
From
The sky.

80.

If the lamppost
And the dog's leg
Ever touch
Then instantaneously
Another lamppost
Is created
Somewhere else
In the world.

81.

We are
All
Actors
Without
A script.

82.

Eggs and spoons
Should be
Left alone
To race
The way they
See fit.

83.

The
Anthropomorphisation
Of animals
Secretly
Disgusts
Them.

84.

Soon
Our minds
Will
Compartmentalise
And we'll be
Aware
In several places
At once.

85.

Trees
Are old
And wise
And we
Should listen
To their
Whisper.

86.

Moon's
Reflection
In water
Makes
The stars
Happy.

87.

We build
Cathedrals
In the sky
To worship
The modern
Age.

88.

Heaven
And hell
Are the same.
Perception
Is different.

89.

Vanity
Is the pretty
Face
Of insecurity.

90.

The tightrope
Balances on thin air.

91.

If there is
No heaven
And hell
Making a pact
With
The devil
Is wise.

92.

If the orange
Is clockwork
The banana
Is mechanical.

93.

Jesus
And his uncle
Visited the
West Country
And met
The Devil.

94.

The glass tree
Has shattered
Fruit.

95.

The
Fortune-teller
Is recounting
The past
In a futuristic
Manner.

96.

The
Jack-in-the-box
Vomits
Its artificial
Joy
Into the air.

97.

The lunatic moon dances
In the sky when all are asleep.

98.

If you place
A shrimp
Next to a
Prawn
Next to a
King prawn
Next to a
Lobster
You have the
Evolution of man
In shellfish form.

99.

When blue
Felt blue
It was happy.

100.

Stop press:
Theoretical Physicist
Under banana tree.
Banana falls on head
- Space-time is curved.

101.

Aliens are
Among us
And sometimes
Are us.
But we don't
Know it.

102.

If you sing
In a void
Your voice
Is beautiful
But meaningless.

103.

The backward clock
Races to catch up
With itself.

104.

Witches' broomsticks
Run on lunar power.

105.

Porcupines are sad
Because they would
Like to hug.

106.

Close your eyes.
Inside your head
Is the true universe.

107.

Frogs and toads
Now love mermaids
Because they got
Fed up with pea soup.

108.

Night watches day
And envies
Its luminosity.

109.

Numbers
Attempt
To instil
Logic
Where there
Is none.

110.

Shoes imprison socks
And laugh
With their tongues out.

111.

She hid her beauty
Under powdered
Layers of insecurity.

112.

Death
Is unimpressed
By physical fitness.

113.

Infinity
Is a never-ending
Story.

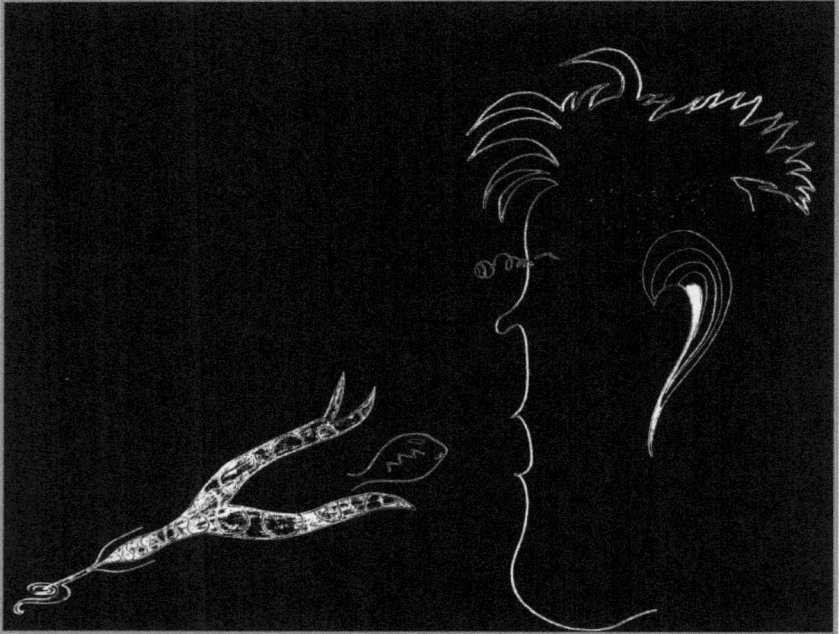

114.

Fly up into
The clouds
At least
Once a day.

115.

The lunatics
Are going to be
Leasing out
Parts of the asylum
For coffee mornings.

116.

Trousers allow
Belts to believe
They are
Serving a purpose.

117.

Mountain ranges
Are the teeth
On the cogs
Of the wheel
Of the earth.

118.

Paper aeroplanes
Fly best thrown
By paper hands.

119.

Lighthouses are signalling
To the alien craft:
"Everyone's gone to sleep.
It's OK to come and have
A look around."

120.

Lost hope
In an impure world
Decaying around the edges.

121.

Uniforms
Wear
The soldiers.

122.

The smug orange
Is both a fruit and a colour.
Tangerine laughs.

123.

Prawns are grey
Till they dress up
And put their
Makeup on.

124.

The man in the mirror
Laughs at my reflection.

125.

Pinocchio's Ears
Were unremarkable.

126.

Sometimes the dictionary
Has to look things up.

127.

What's another
Word for thesaurus?

128.

Perfumes
Are the
Colour-blind test
For the nose.

129.

Ice cream
Is snow
From
Magic mountains.

130.

A diary is a
Good way
Of knowing
What you want
To forget.

131.

Keep life
At its purest.
For at its purest
Life is simple.

132.

When there are
Too many dog coats
In the world
More dogs
Have to be made.

133.

Sun on water
Creates
Water diamonds.

134.

Paper
Would like
To write
A book.

135.

Leopards and giraffes
Are never seen together
Because
Their costumes clash.

135.

Normal
Paving stones
Look at
Crazy paving
With distain.

136.

The road
Less-travelled
Is usually
The one
To take.

137.

Parallel universes
Will soon become
A fact.
But not in all
Universes.

138.

Sadness
Is the body's
Way
Of telling it
To cheer up.

139.

Microwave ovens
Have something
To do with
Time travel.
But nobody
Quite knows
What.

140.

When men do
Doggy-paddle
Dogs must do
Maney-paddle
To even things
Up.

141.

Dry humour
Is no good
In a drought.

142.

If the Big Bang
Made a noise
But nobody was
There to hear it
Was it really
A bang?

143.

Clocks
Have
Wrist watches
They sneakily
Advance
By ten minutes
So as not
To be late.

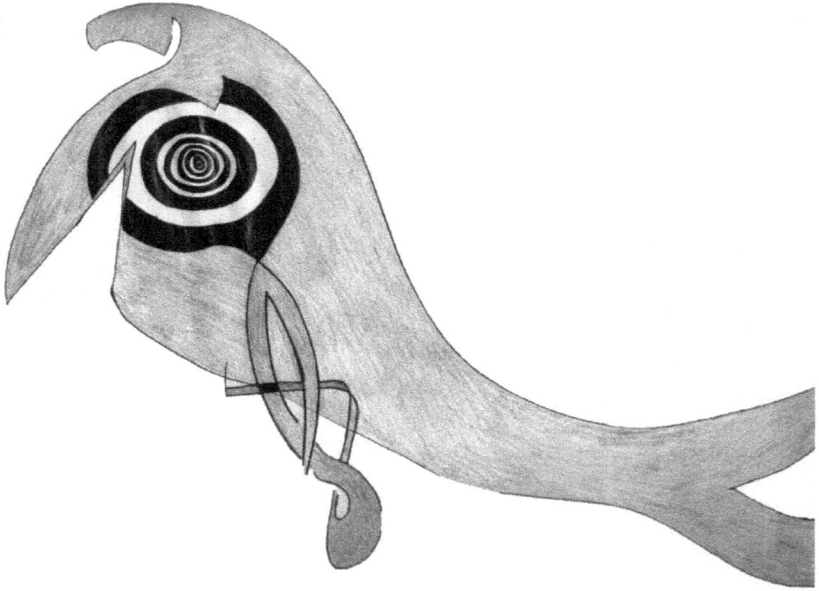

144.

In some countries
Dark humour
Is forbidden
After sundown.

145.

Re-cycling is important
If you haven't owned
A bike for some time.

146.

Some of the
Best cheeses
Are made of
Moon.

147.

Boiled sweets
Are better than
Scrambled
Or fried
Sweets.

148.

Beavers are
The town planners
Of the animal
Kingdom.

149.

Your
Last
Pocket
Has no
Sleeves.

150.

Some things
Float around
When we're
Not looking.

151.

Tables would like
Something
To eat off.

152.

Sometimes
Tubes of nothingness
Are placed
Into mountains
And called
Tunnels.

153.

Jumpers
Only
Jump
In the
Antipodes.

154.

Silences
Add to
The velocity
Of space.

155.

Stairs and lifts
Race each other.

156.

Circles
Are the
Free-thinking
Cousins
Of cubes.

157.

When
Dogs bark
They are
Summoning
Alien
Spacecraft.

158.

Breathing
Gives oxygen
A purpose.

159.

Fire escapes
Are so fires
Can get away quickly
Without being noticed.

160.

When envelopes
Travel
They get homesick.

161.

Colours dance
In
The
Day
And cry
At night.

162.

Weeping willows
Need
To be
Loved.

163.

Ladybirds evolved
From dice.

164.

A full stop
Followed by
A full stop and
Then another
Is the beginning
Of something.

165.

Unicorns
Disappear
When looked at
Directly.

166.

Mouses and mooses
Were related
Before the invention
Of the alphabet.

167.

On very cloudy
Days
The sun plays
Hide and seek
With the moon.

168.

The size of
Men's hats
Is directly
Proportional
To the amount
Of happy thoughts
They have.

169.

Nothingness
Is the glue
That holds
Somethingness
Together.

170.

A forgery
Is just another
Version
Of the
Same thing.

171.

Double agents
Get paid
Time-and-a-half.

172.

The
Back-pocket Kangaroo
Is
Now
Extinct.

173.

Gob-stoppers
Are
Suppositories
For the mouth.

174.

Airports
Should
Float
In the
Sky.

175.

The end of
The sandwich board
Is neigh.

176.

Russian dolls
Like playing
Hide and seek.

177.

Colours laugh
At the
Ludicrousness
Of transparency.

178.

Peas in a pod
Like to
Emphasise
Their individuality.

179.

If you return
To somewhere
You've never been
Time hiccups.

180.

Lobsters
Like
To be
Taken
For walks
In the
Rain.

181.

Ditto dittoed
Keeps
Repeating
Itself.

182.

> Surrealist poetry
>
> Should be
>
> Written
>
> Upside-down.

183.

Bags
Under the eyes
Are
For when
The eyes
Go
On
Holiday.

184.

With what
Do you mend
A hole
That has a
Hole in it?

185.

Some writing
Is not worth
The paper
It is
Written on.

186.

Parallel universes
Are all around us
As much as
Beside us.

187.

He who
Doesn't see
The wall
Is still
A prisoner.

188.

One shouldn't
Wait forever
In front of
Schrödinger's cat flap.

189.

Heaven and hell
Are the
Same place
Seen through
Different
Eyes.

190.

The universe
Without the mind
Is non-existent.
The mind
Without
The universe
Is the universe.

191.

Every bar
Has a little
Old man
In it.

192.

Did
Bananas
Evolve
From
Boomerangs?

193.

Horizontal, vertical
And perpendicular
Went for a walk
But kept bumping
Into
The triangles
Coming the other
Way.

194.

My nose has
No dog.

195.

The table
And the chair
Had a dance
But kept
Falling over
The floor.

196.

Somethingness
Said to
Nothingness:
"You're
So empty."

197.

Nothingness
Said to
Somethingness
"You're so full
Of yourself."

198.

Why
In mathematics
Do
Two nothings
Add up to
Something?

199.

Telephones ring
When they are
Awoken
Suddenly.

200.

Truth
Must be
Told
At all times
Except
When facing
A firing squad.

201.

Aircraft are now
Providing sick bags
For existentialist
Nausea.
These
Are to be
Placed
Over
One's head.

202.

There are no
Greater deceivers
Than
Our five senses.

203.

Art is like
A pickaxe
To the
Chained
And bolted
Gates
Of our
Perception.

NON-SCIENTIFIC

NON-SCIENTIFIC

These thoughts are my own. I have not been coerced nor pressured into making this statement. And I am not being held against my will. I am of sound body and mind and hope that anyone who happens to stumble across this manuscript will take something of value away with them.

These utterances and exclamations were conceived both seventeen years ago and now. The concept for *Being and Somethingness*, as is the case with us ourselves, was lost in time.

By employing *la théorie de l'obscurité* it was important to allow dust from the great nebulous universe to settle in order that this tome could be completely forgotten. And, indeed, it was only by enlisting this regrettably under-used and oft forgotten theory that *Being and Somethingness* could be buried deep underground and disremembered – as the theory dictates it must. This gave the nefarious entity time to mature, evolve, fester and even develop a certain degree of self-pity (that stemmed from it being convinced it had been neglected and left forever).

But, then, however, a series of both simultaneously disheartening and harmony-enhancing events led to the existence (if still only in its embryonic form) of *Being and Somethingness* being recollected and hence retrieved from its subterranean vault. Huzzah!

It should be noted, as only a slight aside, that many things are often buried…

Thus, some of which is between these covers was dug up and brushed down, and brought to you on a silver platter of love and mystery – a bit like a pig's head on a platter with a red apple in its mouth, if the head represents the universe and the apple represents the key to unlocking its secrets, namely, *Being and Somethingness*.

So, then, the object of this final treatise is to pull strands together while developing other themes that may lead one to explore unchartered alleyways that could prove fruitful in preparation for the next phase...

------● ● ●------

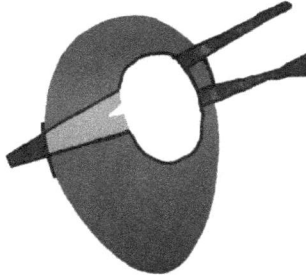

The inner pulsating essence and meaning of the universe can only be tapped into to any meaningful extent through art, meditation (of a specific kind), through either sensory deprivation or sensory enhancement, via the exploration of numerology, and via an appreciation of the philosophy of sign recognition and symbolism.

*

Chaos theory can only take us so far in appreciating order in disorder. It is our task to also seek meaning in meaninglessness. Sometimes we feel, do we not, that a hallucinatory or revelatory insight or understanding is on the verge of presenting itself to us. Then the moment passes, the feeling is gone, and beautiful randomness is restored. These moments must be entered into (using one of the aforementioned techniques), grasped, captured, benefited from and seen as a key.

GENERAL AND SPECIFIC
SOMETHINGNESS AND NOTHINGNESS

The oneness in everything should not be open to dispute. The, so-called, tangible and the intangible, the solid and the fluid, are all at all times always in flux and in search of greater identity, essence, and 'confidence' in their essentialness of entity.

As we are aware, to observe certain elements is to alter their essence. Direct observation can result in complete disappearance, or it can lead to incomprehensible inaccuracies. For example, the more precisely the position of some particle is determined, the less precisely its momentum can be known, and vice versa.

To observe or scrutinise certain things too closely, too directly, is to contribute to their disappearance and diminution of essentialness. Since all and everything, in a sense, is one – made from the same space and vibrations – the question must be broached as to whether this is also the case for sentient beings?

The too direct consideration or observation from without can, as far as we can ascertain, result in the partial evaporation of what we shall call, and have been calling, the essentialness[1] of something. The extent to which this evaporation can occur is partly dependent upon the solidity and self-manifested and self-perpetuated distractedness of the organism. And there will always be – to a greater or lesser degree – an element of culpability, and usually at a subconscious level, in this process of evaporation.

It is during these sustained periods of spiralling, thus far inexplicable, evolutions of evaporation, that somethingness becomes nothingness – (this is a gradual process – and up until the end point reversible).

*

is variously known as the 'incorporeal' or the 'soul', for
example. We have purposefully shied away from using such
terms that have a religious or quasi-mystical connotation…
That said, certain religions teach that non-biological entities
(such as rivers and mountains) possess souls. This latter belief is
called animism.

The ultimate and most supreme example of anti-somethingness is a
'black hole'. A black hole is one or all of three things:

- It can be where all of the most densely concentrated mass of nothingness in the universe is to be found. A nothingness that is held together by a kind of 'glue' that has an identity and an almost undeterminable vibratory quality which encourages all the disparate foundations of nothingness to be gelled together.

- A black hole can also be a means by which we will be able to time travel.

- And, finally, a black hole can be the porthole and subsequent channel that will lead us through to parallel universes. Parallel universes in which 'being' and 'somethingness' could possibly already be merged.

Hence, then, in a universe where big is small (i.e. there is no unified theory of everything, for example); where mere observation can cause the onset of an inexplicable process of degradation towards invisibility and/or the inaccurate and inconsistent accumulation of data; and where the distinct lines between the end of one entity and the beginning of another are, and should be, blurred – surely, then, we are existing in a time where 'being and somethingness' are establishing the way forward. A way that is a more accurately accepting anti-analytical approach to seeing and being a part of the whole and the hole (for there is no greater something than nothing).

Søren Kierkegaard stated that we should not reflect ourselves out of reality. And as an extension we should consider that nothing be 'reflected' out of reality. We have an identity and a perceived reality, and these alter constantly as we move, progress, consider and interpret. Our reality, as with any reality, is in constant – we shall utilise the term 'elastic' – elastic flux. As with a sheet of bendable mirror-like metal, or a distorted circus mirror, reality bends, wobbles, advances and retracts… Truth and reality meld as we seek and blink our way through the bright sunlight of perception. At times we are indistinguishable from our surroundings and vice versa.

To illustrate melting perception and altering reality I shall cite a simple example that occurred today. I went into a second hand shop here in Spain. I wished to purchase a hat because February is a cold month. I rummaged until I eventually found something that I thought convivial. It was a grey, mainly grey, and orange trimmed woollen hat. Very tasteful and practical I can hear those of you who know about such matters say. But wait! On its side were stitched the letters, in orange, A.E.. Now, the person who I was with – on seeing my new old hat said that the letters could easily be unstitched. Whereas the first thought that had occurred to me on seeing the letters on the woollen hat concerned how one changes one's name by deed poll.

NUMBERS

We can safely assume that numbers are at the core of understanding the universe.

*

The most significant of all the numbers is zero… As with the black hole – anywhere, and under any circumstance, in the universe where nothing can be expressed as something or something can be expressed as nothing we must consider as being a significant monicker[2].

In one sense zero can be said to be the fullest, weightiest and most substantive of all numbers since it is the only number that is indivisible. It is neither positive nor negative. And crucially, some might say paradoxically, everything (the universe) has stemmed from nothing, zero, and yet has continued to grow. Hence, in this sense, zero – nothingness – is the creator, the enlarger, the expander. From nothingness comes somethingness and beyond.

To comprehend the intuitive and non-scientific essentialness of the universe one must pay close consideration to the characteristics and behaviour of the number zero[3]. For not to do so would leave us un-whole and unprepared for the next phase.

2– 'monicker' is said to be possibly an alteration from Irish *Shelta münnik*. It originally meant a mark left by a tramp on a building or fence to indicate that he had been there; a tramp's moniker, therefore, identified him in a similar way to a signature… It is thought to be the origins of graffiti identification signatures, known as 'tags'.

Here we have chosen to use it in the sense of it being emblematic or symbolic (an identification mark, if you will) of something else substantial being present or occurring.

3 – 'zero' in pre-Islamic time the word ṣifr (Arabic ص فر) had the meaning 'empty'. Ṣifr evolved to mean zero when it was used to translate śūnya (Sanskrit: शून्य) from India. The first known English use of zero was in 1598.

The Italian mathematician Fibonacci (c.1170–1250), who grew up in North Africa and is credited with introducing the decimal system to Europe, used the term zephyrum.

As the decimal zero and its new mathematics spread from the Arabic world to Europe in the Middle Ages, words derived from ṣifr and zephyrus came to refer to calculation, as well as to privileged knowledge and secret codes...

According to Ifrah, "in thirteenth-century Paris, a 'worthless fellow' was called a cifre en algorisme: an arithmetical nothing." From ṣifr also came the French chiffre.

By 1740 BCE, the Egyptians had a symbol for zero in accounting texts. The symbol was nfr, and means beautiful.

It is interesting is it not that for many centuries, and also on the earlier typewriters, there was no distinction made between how one wrote the letter 'O' from the digit '0'. Therein possibly lies a subconscious bringing to light of a suppressed expression of surprise or marvel – as in 'Oh', or 'Oo'.

*

The second most important number after zero is infinity, represented by ∞. The earliest attestable accounts of mathematical infinity come from Zeno of Elea (c. 490 BCE – c. 430 BCE). He was a pre-Socratic Greek philosopher from southern Italy and a member of the Eleatic School founded by Parmenides. Aristotle considered him to be the inventor of the dialectic. However, he is best known for his *paradoxes*, which were "immeasurably subtle and profound", according to Bertrand Russell.

In 1584, the Italian philosopher and astronomer Giordano Bruno proposed an unbounded universe in *On the Infinite Universe and Worlds*, stating that: "Innumerable suns exist; innumerable earths revolve around these suns in a manner similar to the way the seven planets revolve around our sun. Living beings inhabit these worlds."

Cosmologists have long sought to discover whether infinity exists in our physical universe. Are there an infinite number of stars? Does the universe have infinite volume? Does space continue ad infinitum? Note that the question of being infinite is logically separate from the question of having boundaries. The two-dimensional surface of the Earth, for example, is finite, yet has no edge. By travelling in a straight line, therefore, one will eventually return to the exact spot from which one set off.

The universe, some have argued, at least in principle, might have a similar topology. If this were the case, one would eventually return to one's starting point after travelling in a straight line through the universe for long enough.

If, however, conversely, as we believe to be the case, the universe is not curved like a sphere and instead has a 'flat' topology, it could well be infinite... The curvature, or otherwise, of the universe can be measured through multipole moments in the spectrum of the cosmic background radiation. As to date, as we suspected, analysis of the radiation patterns recorded by the WMAP spacecraft suggests that the universe has a non-curved topology.

And this, of course, is consistent with an infinite physical universe. Indeed it is also consistent with the multiverse hypothesis, explained by, for example, astrophysicists such as Michio Kaku, who posits that there are an infinite number and variety of universes. The multiverse (or meta-universe) is the hypothetical set of infinite or finite possible universes (including the Universe we consistently experience) that together comprise everything that exists: the entirety of space, time, matter, and energy as well as the physical laws and constants that describe them. The various universes within the multiverse are sometimes called parallel universes or 'alternate universes'.

And this neatly brings us onto our next field of consideration, that of the role and reason for Symbols. For, as we will advance, symbols and signs come from one of two sources. Either from our grand, all but forgotten or buried, consciousness, or, via seepages into our universe from other parallel universes...

*

Briefly, however, prior to moving on to our next area of non-analysis[4] we should spend a moment mentioning the third most

---

4 – 'non-analysis' is a term we use since we consider that analytical thought frequently runs as a halt or a counter to illumination via intuitive insight. One must be open, observant, insightful at a semi-unconscious or instinctive level – and not, so to speak 'overthink' one's thoughts; while maintaining a degree of near-constant 'meditational' appreciation of nature, the universe, and what it is willing to 'give' us (from its essentialness).

---

important number: Pi.

Pi is a marvellous, magical, mystological and stupendous number. And it not just in the sky but all around us throughout the universe. As with 'zero' and 'infinity' it also holds secrets that require unlocking[5].

It is not interesting that the Great Pyramid at Giza seems to approximate pi. The vertical height of the pyramid has the same relationship to the perimeter of its base as the radius of a circle has to its circumference.

Time should also be set aside to contemplate that the 359th, 360th, and 361st digits of pi respectively are 360...

Also, noteworthy is the fact that thirty-nine decimal places of pi suffice for computing the circumference of a circle girding the known universe with an error no greater than the radius of a hydrogen atom.

It seems that essentialness, and its secrets, was also sought by Leonardo da Vinci (1452-1519) and artist Albrecht Durer (1471-1528) who both briefly worked on 'squaring the circle', or approximating pi.

Fig 1.

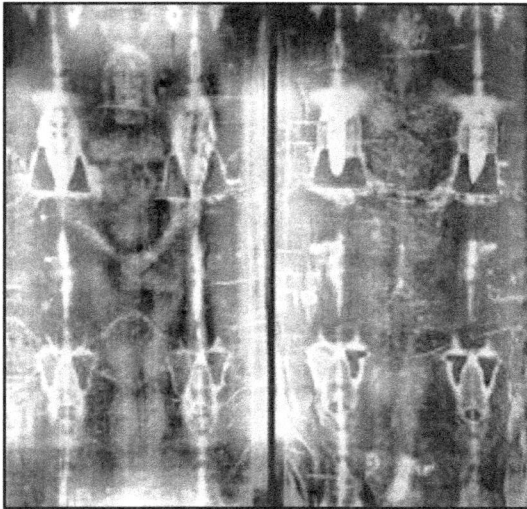

The Turin Shroud.

We mention the following in a light-hearted manner – as a gentle anecdotal aside. A Japanese gentleman, who still holds the record, memorised 42,195 places of pi. He is known as the pi champion. Fascinatingly some scholars speculate that Japanese is better suited than other languages to memorising sequences of numbers. His favourite food, which possibly attributed to his concentration, was a kind of sliced apple speciality in a circular pastry type of form – it being circular is of course very appropriate.

*

This said we must now return to the matter in hand. This has necessarily only been a brief look at Pi – a more in depth non-analysis will come at a later date, when we have completed our on-going research.

SYMBOLS AND SYMBOLISM

It would be trite to state that symbols are symbolic? But how else can one express the significance and meaning of the symbols that one identifies either correctly or incorrectly as being significant in our necessitous unravelling of the space-time paradigm.

Unfortunately there are no doors or locks to be snapped apart or broken down. All is circuitous. And indeed the final key can be arrived at via a means of comprehension in space-time combined with an understanding of the mythological and pre-historical insights arrived at by our ancestors. Ancestors who – in the Mesopotamian world, the Chinese world, the Celtic-cum-Pagan world and the Mesoamerican and South American world – were able to conceive of and 'partially', 'segmentally', understand the greater intuitive non-linear laws that prevail. And once accessed, these laws (although 'laws' is a term too loaded with a sense of rigidity), these *illuminations* (if accepted and understood) were given higher significance than any ruler of a fiefdom or kingdom. Rightly so.

Unfortunately – both for these cultures, and for us – the illuminations that were revealed were fragmented, fragmented or fragments of the whole. True, on occasion ('on occasion' here meaning over decades if not centuries) several elements were able to be pieced together and great leaps forward in 'advancement' were achieved. But these shards were never built upon to any fundamental extent. Either because the civilisations died out, the knowledge (and more importantly how to access it) was not passed on, or crucially because warring cultures or cultures that were unaware of another's existence, due to geographical separation, did not share and meld their enlightenments together.

Of course not all the mystological insights and discernments have been mislaid, re-entombed, enshrouded in misinterpretation or occasionally thrown in our direction, knowingly, with concealed misdirection and sleight of hand.

Fig 2. Illustrates a number of noteworthy cross-cultural and cross-millennial pyramids.

Fig 2.

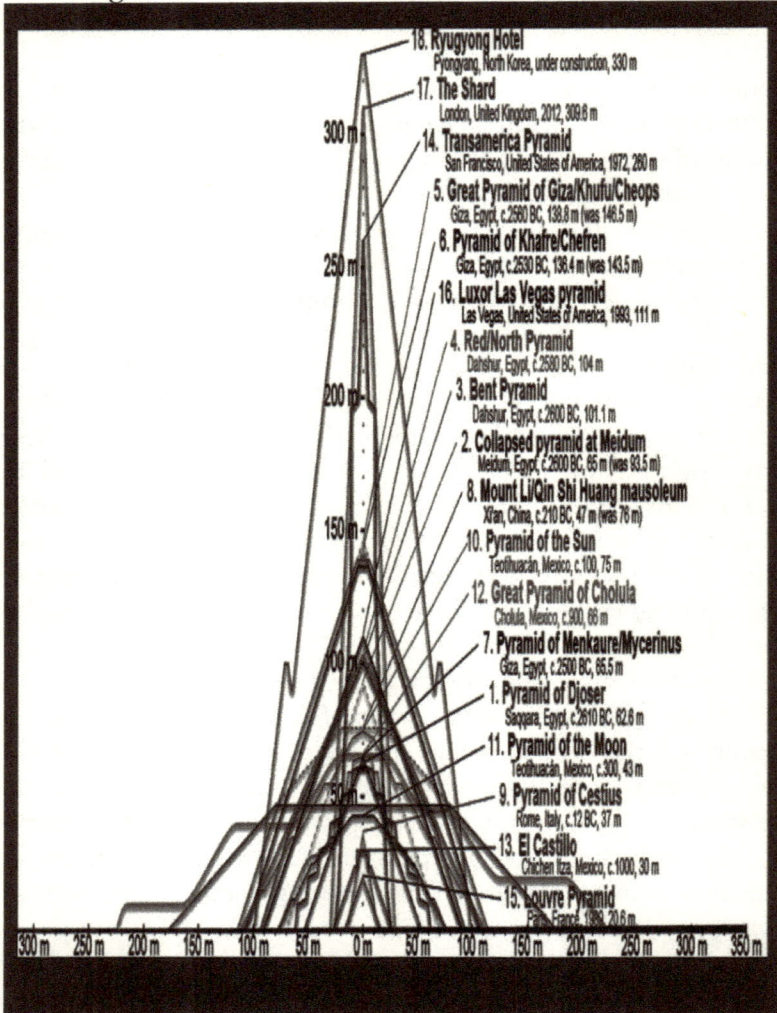

18. Ryugyong Hotel
Pyongyang, North Korea, under construction, 330 m

17. The Shard
London, United Kingdom, 2012, 309.6 m

14. Transamerica Pyramid
San Francisco, United States of America, 1972, 260 m

5. Great Pyramid of Giza/Khufu/Cheops
Giza, Egypt, c.2560 BC, 138.8 m (was 146.5 m)

6. Pyramid of Khafre/Chefren
Giza, Egypt, c.2530 BC, 136.4 m (was 143.5 m)

16. Luxor Las Vegas pyramid
Las Vegas, United States of America, 1993, 111 m

4. Red/North Pyramid
Dahshur, Egypt, c.2580 BC, 104 m

3. Bent Pyramid
Dahshur, Egypt, c.2600 BC, 101.1 m

2. Collapsed pyramid at Meidum
Meidum, Egypt, c.2600 BC, 65 m (was 93.5 m)

8. Mount Li/Qin Shi Huang mausoleum
Xi'an, China, c.210 BC, 47 m (was 76 m)

10. Pyramid of the Sun
Teotihuacán, Mexico, c.100, 75 m

12. Great Pyramid of Cholula
Cholula, Mexico, c.900, 66 m

7. Pyramid of Menkaure/Mycerinus
Giza, Egypt, c.2500 BC, 65.5 m

1. Pyramid of Djoser
Saqqara, Egypt, c.2610 BC, 62.6 m

11. Pyramid of the Moon
Teotihuacán, Mexico, c.300, 43 m

9. Pyramid of Cestius
Rome, Italy, c.12 BC, 37 m

13. El Castillo
Chichen Itza, Mexico, c.1000, 30 m

15. Louvre Pyramid
Paris, France, 1989, 20.6 m

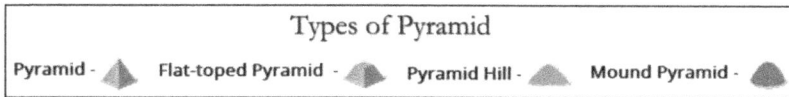

Types of Pyramid			
Pyramid - 🔺	Flat-toped Pyramid - 🔺	Pyramid Hill - 🔺	Mound Pyramid - 🔺

*

Jung referred to the 'collective unconsciousness' and Freud referred to 'archaic remnants'. Here we shall refer to it as 'what we know we don't know'.

Fig3.

Fig 3. Illustration by Sandro Botticelli (made between 1480 and 1490) depicting the structure of hell according to Dante Alighieri's *Divine Comedy*. Carl Gustav Jung stated that among every culture hell represents the disturbing aspect of the collective unconscious.

Jung states that " …in addition to our immediate consciousness… which we believe to be the only empirical psyche… there exists a second psychic system of a collective, universal, and impersonal nature which is identical in all individuals. This collective unconscious does not develop individually but is inherited. It consists of pre-existent forms, the archetypes, which can only become conscious secondarily and which give definite form to certain psychic contents."

This was a theme that I covered in my novel *The Cubist's House*. Namely that there is some form of grand consciousness that from time to time is tapped into and utilised, and can propel mankind onto a more advanced path. Whether that is in the form of Pyramids, or whether it is in the form of Hell. However to our mind Jung's idea of there being similar cross-cultural ideas of a hell we would state from our vantage point are more probably mass veiled unconscious representations and misinterpretations of one of the fundamental aspects of the space-time intrigue. Namely the black hole, the ultimate of all nothingnesses.

In linguistically, artistically and scientifically, shall we say, more primitive eras it is understandable, is it not, that blackness and nothingness – in other words, the antithesis of being and somethingness – be seen as the epitome of pain, loss of identity, and the definitive and unequivocal evaporation of the essentialness of self. Hell. But comprehensible though it is, it was (and still is) inaccurate. We all, as part of our collective unconscious, what we could also deem our subconscious awareness, have a concept of the void. And that void, or frightening darkness, has always – almost exclusively – be seen as hades.

To be *aware* finally of the correct interpretation of the symbol, firstly, of the embandaged knowledge of the centre of nothingness, and secondly, as a consequence, to be able to act upon that knowledge is, and can be, a step forward in preparation for the ensuing phase.

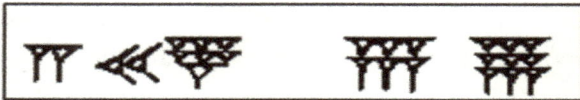

*

We allow, indeed invite, the reader to make his or her own conclusions. But we hope, and anticipate, that read in the correct manner this text will aid in the appreciation of symbols, in the unveiling of masks, in the halting of evaporation, and the preparation for the next phase. '…seek and thee shall look for', 'discover and thee shall find'.

THE WORD

When the UFOs appear to us and the aliens come – are we tapping into the reality of another dimension? Another dimension where we are/would be the aliens.

Alien abductions are on the increase, UFO sightings are becoming more frequent, expressions such as 'I knew you were going to say that' have blown out of all proportions, and the phenomenon of crop circles has certainly focused the mind in recent times.

We must be vigilant, in the sense of being ready and prepared. And for those who have not already begun to seek their own essentialness as part of the whole essentialness, we strongly suggest that they commence immediately before it's too late.

Keys will be revealed, have already been revealed. But it is only by being willing and knowing how to read those keys and indeed where and when those keys could be revealed that we will be able to tap into the knowledge that is already there (that may in all probability at one point have been lost).

Reading the signs, being artistically open, and appreciating that 'nothing' is the greatest of all 'somethings' that we have, will aid our transformation into true preparedness for the next phase.

SYMBOLS, SIGNS AND
MYSTOLOGICAL REVELATIONS –
AND HOW TO FIND THEM AND EVALUATE THEIR
SIGNIFICANCE

The follow-up to this edition will concentrate on illuminated access and key recognition.

How to determine a line of potentially valuable insight, how to trace it back to as close to its 'source' as is possible, how to distinguish substantial medieval and pre-historical artefacts and wisdom from that which is hoax or mischievous buffoonery (corn circles, for example; which are real and which are fake? And what do we mean by 'real and 'fake' in any case?).

In our research we are on the brink of being able to unequivocally prove whether Jesus set foot in Glastonbury or not. We are in the process of considering the Arthurian legend, Celtic legend, the symbolism of lizards, Bobby Fisher and the significance or otherwise of Chess grand masters, and so much more that we feel that several breakthroughs (that we shall reveal in our follow-up book) are within our grasp.

Oh, and for a little light relief (that is most probably best seen as an 'infomercial', but with no selling involved) we shall be recounting the story of when Charlie Chaplin surreptitiously entered a Charlie Chaplin look-a-like contest and came third (see the beginning of my novel Lines Within The Circle for the not too dissimilar account concerning the invisible man).

But this of course will merely be to give the reader a momentary breather. Before the serious business of preparing ourselves (and indeed others) for the next phase continues.

More importantly we will be revealing for the first time our belief that rather than Da Vinci (or any spurious links to the man) it was the surrealists: Buñuel, Magritte, Gérard de Nerval, Man Ray, and Duchamp, for example, as well as Salvador Dalí who – to a large extent unbeknownst to themselves – had tapped into certain strands of consciousness that if followed and extended could, we suspect, lead to some significant openings to gateways to illumination.

Hence, then, this, as well as the other aforementioned themes, and more, will be fully explored, anti-analysed and non-scientifically scrutinised through the prism of guided and independently verified research.

The follow-up in this series will be titled:

THE DA DALÍ CODE

For advanced orders of a limited edition numbered and signed copy please contact the website:

www.jeanbonnin.com

PEACE****LOVE****ENERGY****INFINITY
FOREVER

NOTES AND ACKNOWLEDGEMENTS

I wish to thank:

- The *theory of random leakage*
- The Who's 1970 appearance at the Isle of Wight festival
- Repetition – the enablement of repetition in art, culture, possibly above all in music to create 'hypnotic drone'… This form of self-acceptingly-induced meditational hypnosis can open one up to the potential for what we shall call *enlightenment* – but what we really mean are glimpses of the *revelatory picture*.
- Repetition
- Lynn Bonnin
- Rolfe Llewellyn

V1

Jean Bonnin
Majorca, Spain
8th February 2015

This is my fourth published work, though sixth completed work…

* Madame P.P. de la Grange   ** Professor Ran Dieky

www.redeggpublishing.com

www.ingramcontent.com/pod-product-compliance
Lightning Source LLC
Chambersburg PA
CBHW030110070426
42448CB00036B/632